WORSHIP WITH ME

At the

SYNAGOGUE

By Shalini Vallepur

BookLife
PUBLISHING

©2020
BookLife Publishing Ltd.
King's Lynn
Norfolk PE30 4LS

A catalogue record for this
book is available from the
British Library.

ISBN: 978-1-78637-972-6

Written by:
Shalini Vallepur

Edited by:
Madeline Tyler

Designed by:
Jasmine Pointer

Photo Credits

All images courtesy of Shutterstock.com.
With thanks to Getty Images, Thinkstock Photo
and iStockphoto.

Header font throughout – Shtonado. Front Cover – Shtonado,
miumi, robuart, Tartila, Ilya Bolotov, naum. 4 – Magicleaf,
asantosg. 5 – Roman Yanushevsky. 8 – HappyPictures, illustratioz.
9 – Brajcev. 10 – Macrovector, yhelfman. 11 – Spiroview Inc. 12
– David Cohen 156. 13 – Liron Peer, romawka. 14 – Bachrach44
[Public domain] https://commons.wikimedia.org/wiki/File:Ner_
tamid.jpg. 16 – Anatolir. 17 – BooHoo, Donna Ellen Coleman.
18 – Valen Zi, Lucia Fox. 19 – Lindasj22. 22 – Thebirdss.

CONTENTS

Words that look like __this__ can be found in the glossary on page 24.

WORSHIP

With Me

Shalom! That means 'hello' in <u>Hebrew</u>. I'm a rabbi at a synagogue and I'll be showing you around.

Have you ever been to a synagogue? A synagogue is a building of <u>worship</u> for followers of Judaism. Judaism began around 4,000 years ago in the Middle East.

Rabbis are teachers of Judaism. They help people in the <u>community</u> and lead worship at the synagogue. There are different types of Judaism around the world that follow different things, but all Jewish people worship at the synagogue.

Many people come to the synagogue to study or meet friends.

Welcome to the SYNAGOGUE

This is the Star of David. It is a <u>symbol</u> of Judaism. Most synagogues will have a Star of David on the outside.

Synagogues usually have at least 12 windows to let in lots of light during prayer.

There are different types of Judaism around the world. This means that some synagogues can look very different to others.

INSIDE
the Synagogue

We worship in a room called the sanctuary. In some synagogues, men put a <u>kippah</u> on their head. Some women may cover their hair with a kippah or a scarf.

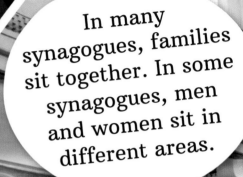

In many synagogues, families sit together. In some synagogues, men and women sit in different areas.

Kippot (kippahs)

The city of Jerusalem is very important in Judaism. When it is possible, we make sure that the sanctuary is built facing Jerusalem so that all prayers are directed towards it.

The ARK

The Aron Hakodesh, or the ark, is usually at the front of the sanctuary. The ark is one of the most important parts of the synagogue.

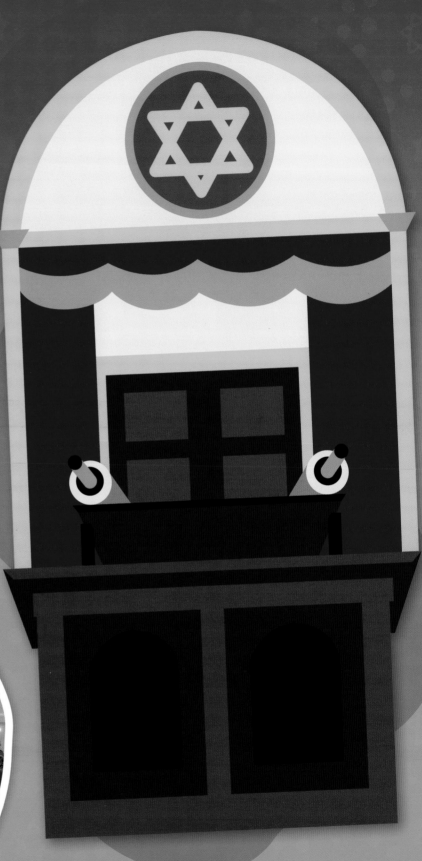

Some arks are decorated, while others are very simple. They are usually wooden and most have doors and curtains. When the doors of the ark are opened, everybody must stand.

Curtain

The TORAH

The Torah <u>scrolls</u> are kept inside the ark. Each Torah scroll is carefully written out by a <u>scribe</u>.

The Torah is usually written in Hebrew.

The Torah scrolls are usually taken out of the ark three times a week to be read. A cloth called a mantel is sometimes used to protect the Torah scrolls from getting damaged.

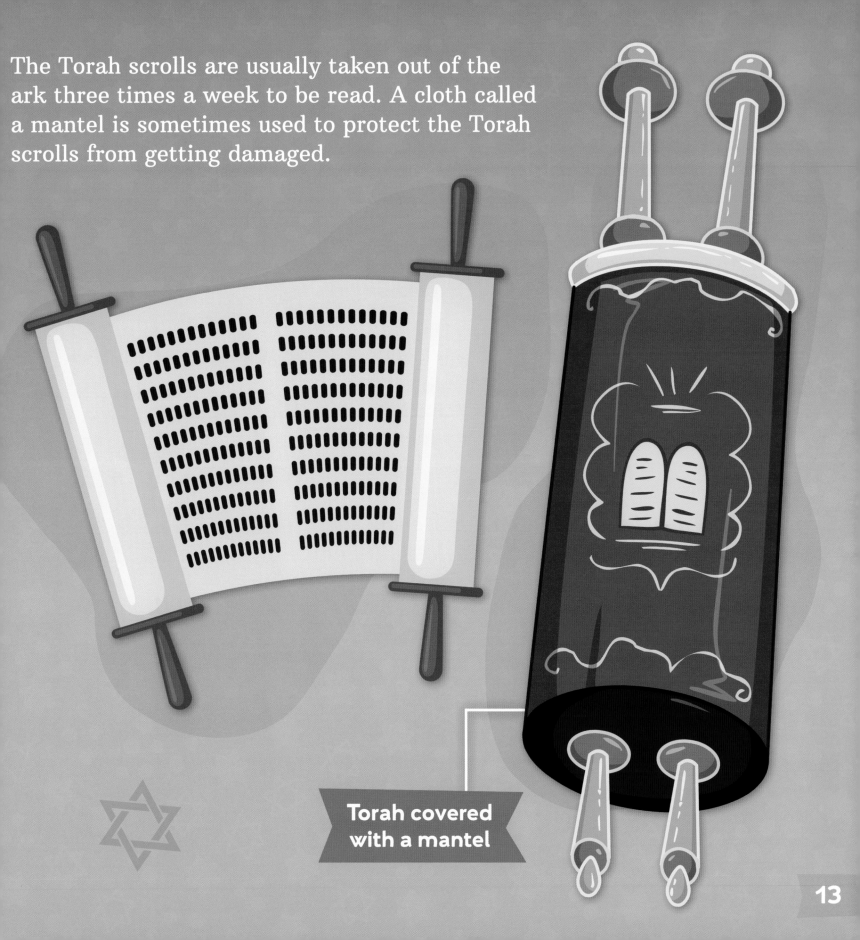

Torah covered with a mantel

NER TAMID

The Ner Tamid hangs above the ark. It is a lamp that is kept on at all times. Ner Tamid means 'eternal light'.

The light in a Ner Tamid used to come from a flame, but now most synagogues use light bulbs.

The MENORAH

The Ner Tamid's light reminds us of the golden <u>menorah</u> that burned years ago in Jerusalem. Some synagogues have a menorah in the sanctuary as well as the Ner Tamid.

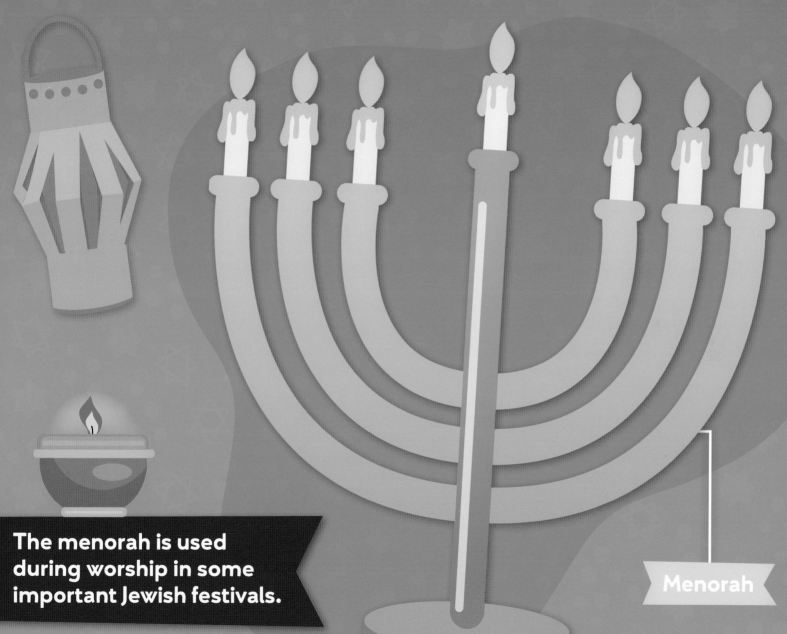

The menorah is used during worship in some important Jewish festivals.

Menorah

PRAYING

Praying is an important part of worship. There are three prayers that are said every day.

Shacharit – the morning prayer

Minchah – the afternoon prayer

Maariv – the evening prayer

Many people pray at home, but worshippers try to pray at the synagogue with friends and family whenever they can. Some prayers are <u>recited</u>. Other times, a rabbi reads from the Torah or a prayer book.

Yad

When I read from the Torah, I use a yad to help me. The yad is a pointed tool and it means I don't have to touch and damage the Torah.

SHABBAT

Challah

Shabbat is a very holy time of the week. It begins at sunset on Friday and ends at sunset on Saturday. Shabbat is a time of rest and worship. Many families go to the synagogue for the weekly Shabbat service.

Families eat a special type of bread called challah during Shabbat.

During the service, the Torah is removed from the ark and brought to a platform called the bimah. The rabbi usually leads the service.

Shabbat is also known as Sabbath.

Torah Scroll
Unrolled to Exodus 36, referencing the building of the tabernacle.

Reading Table
Podiums used for Torah reading have

YOM KIPPUR

Yom Kippur is celebrated after Rosh Hashanah, the Jewish New Year. Many adults <u>fast</u> during Yom Kippur. Girls who are over the age of 12 and boys who are over the age of 13 may also fast.

Many people wear white clothes during Yom Kippur.

Everybody goes to the synagogue to pray. Many people will pray alone, but at the end of the day everybody gathers to recite prayers together.

Tallitot

Men sometimes wear prayer shawls called tallitot. White robes called kittel are also worn.

The JEWISH Calendar

We use the Jewish calendar to work out the dates of religious events. The calendar follows the patterns of the Moon and the Sun. There are usually 12 months in a year. A <u>Jewish leap year</u> has 13 months.

The Jewish calendar is a different length to the <u>Gregorian calendar</u>. The dates of Jewish festivals change on the Gregorian calendar every year.

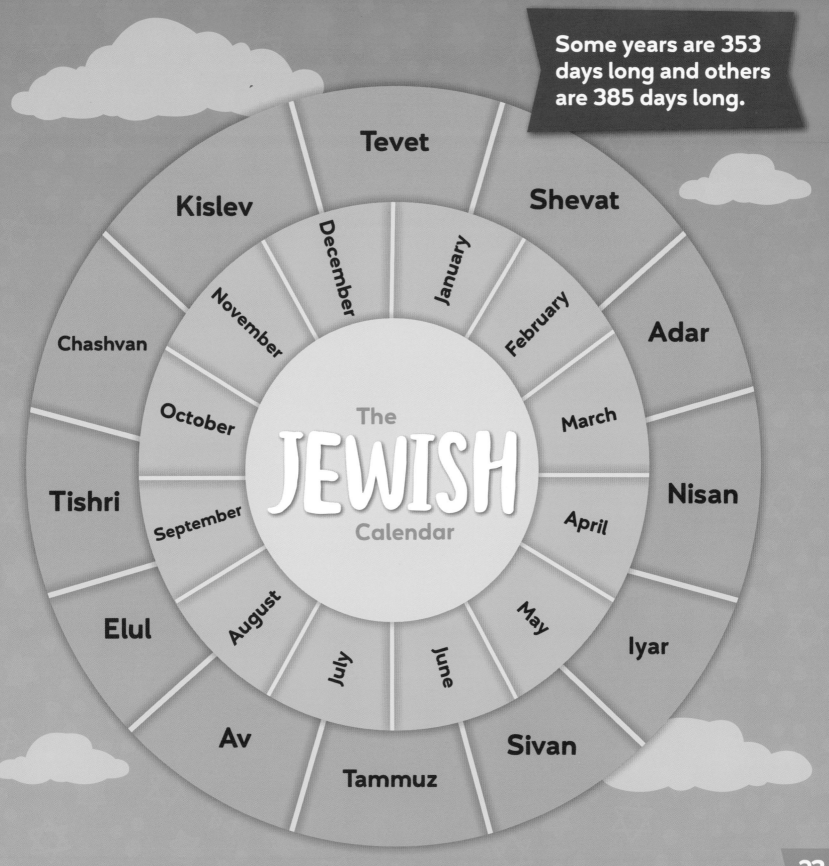

Some years are 353 days long and others are 385 days long.

The **JEWISH** Calendar

Tevet — December
Shevat — January
Adar — February
Nisan — March / April
Iyar — May
Sivan — June
Tammuz — July
Av — August
Elul — September
Tishri — October
Chashvan — November
Kislev — December

23

GLOSSARY

community	a group of people who are connected by something
eternal	having no beginning or end; lasting forever
fast	to not eat or drink, often for religious reasons
Gregorian calendar	the calendar that is used around the world that starts with the month of January
Hebrew	a common language spoken by Jewish people
Jewish leap year	a year in the Jewish calendar that has 13 months and occurs seven times in a 19-year cycle
kippah	a small hat that is usually worn by Jewish men during worship
menorah	a candlestick with seven or nine branches that is used for worship in Judaism
recited	to have spoken words aloud, often from memory
scribe	a person who is trained to write out sacred texts in Judaism
scrolls	big rolls of paper with writing on them
symbol	a thing that is used as a sign for something else
worship	a religious act where a person shows their love for a god or gods

INDEX